WHAT SHOULD I DO?   WHAT SHOULD I DO?

COMMUNITY · CONNECTIONS

?

WHAT SHOULD I DO?
IF A STRANGER COMES NEAR
BY WIL MARA

CHERRY LAKE Publishing

Published in the United States of America by Cherry Lake Publishing
Ann Arbor, Michigan
www.cherrylakepublishing.com

Content Adviser: Karen Sheehan, MD, MPH, Children's Memorial Hospital, Chicago, Illinois

Photo Credits: Cover, ©Suzanne Tucker/Shutterstock, Inc.; page 5, ©SoleilC/Shutterstock, Inc.; page 7, ©Valeriy Lebedev/Shutterstock, Inc.; page 9, ©Janina Dierks/Shutterstock, Inc.; page 11, ©Onedayoneimage/Dreamstime.com; page 13, ©Design Pics Inc./Alamy; page 15, ©Martin Novak/Shutterstock, Inc.; page 17, ©naluwan/Shutterstock, Inc.; page 19, ©Dean Mitchell/Shutterstock, Inc.; page 21, ©Monkey Business Images/Dreamstime.com.

LIBRARY OF CONGRESS CATALOGING-IN-PUBLICATION DATA
Mara, Wil.
  What should I do if a stranger comes near?/by Wil Mara.
    p. cm.—(Community connections)
  Includes bibliographical references and index.
  ISBN-13: 978-1-61080-049-5 (lib. bdg.)
  ISBN-10: 1-61080-049-4 (lib. bdg.)
  1. Children and strangers—Juvenile literature. 2. Safety education—Juvenile literature.
  3. Kidnapping—Prevention—Juvenile literature. I. Title. II. Series.
  HQ784.S8M37 2011
  613.6083—dc22   2011012313

Cherry Lake Publishing would like to acknowledge the work of The Partnership for 21st Century Skills. Please visit *www.21stcenturyskills.org* for more information.

Printed in the United States of America
Corporate Graphics Inc.
July 2011
CLFA09

IF A STRANGER COMES NEAR

CONTENTS

WHAT SHOULD I DO?

STRANGERS ARE EVERYWHERE

Imagine you are playing outside by yourself. Someone comes up and starts talking to you. This person is an adult. He is also a **stranger**. You could be in trouble. What would you do?

Playing outside is fun, but you should always keep an eye out for strangers.

The stranger might seem very friendly. He might even say that he has something to show you or give you. He might try to **lure** you with candy. Or he might say that he has a pet he wants you to see. This might sound okay to you. But it is not.

Do not talk to a stranger who tries to get you to come near his car.

Take a minute to look around every time you go outside. Are there any strangers nearby? How close are they? Are they sitting in cars? Are they watching you? It is always a good idea to know who is around you.

A STRANGER COULD MEAN DANGER

Most strangers do not want to hurt you. But you still want to keep yourself safe. That is why you need to learn what to do if a stranger comes near.

Strangers will often be bigger and older than you. This means they will be much stronger than you.

A stranger might look like a nice person, but that doesn't mean you should talk to him.

A stranger could grab you and **abduct** you. He could cover your mouth so you could not scream. He could make you get into a car and drive away with you. He could take you someplace where you could not **escape**.

Be sure to stay close to a parent or other trusted adult when you are in a crowded place.

Can you think of some places where a stranger might talk to you? What about a restaurant? Or at a baseball game? What about when you're on the computer? Do you think that some places are safer than others?

11

WHAT TO DO WHEN A STRANGER COMES NEAR

It is okay to feel scared if a stranger comes close to you. That is the way you are supposed to feel. But you should also think about what you need to do next. If a stranger talks to you, do not **reply**.

Think about how to stay safe if a stranger tries to talk to you.

13

Run to an adult you know and trust. Tell that person about the stranger.

Run away from the stranger if no one you know is nearby. Run inside a building if you can. Be sure to lock the door.

Adults you know and trust will be happy to help you stay safe.

Defend yourself if a stranger tries to grab you. Kick and punch the stranger as hard as you can. Then run away as soon as you can get free.

You should also yell for help. Be as loud as you can. Other people will hear you and come running. Yelling might also scare the stranger away.

Yell for help if a stranger is scaring you.

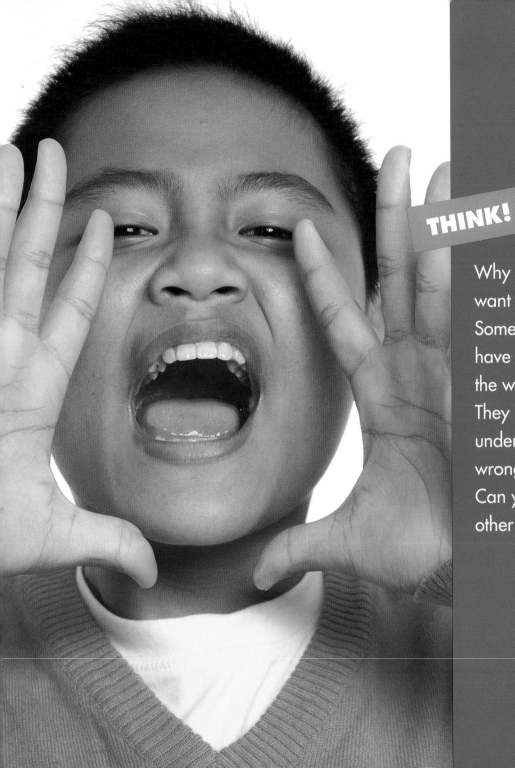

THINK!

Why would anyone want to hurt a child? Some people might have problems with the way they think. They might not understand that it is wrong to hurt others. Can you think of other reasons?

17

NO STRANGERS, NO DANGERS

There are ways to avoid problems with strangers. The best one is to keep away from them in the first place. Always stay close to adults you know and trust. A stranger will not come near you if you are with other people.

Strangers will not bother children who are with their parents. Instead, they look for children who are alone.

CREATE!

Ask your parents to help create a plan for you to follow if a stranger ever bothers you. Practice the plan over and over. Then you can be sure it will work if you ever need to use it.

19

Don't go out of your house or your school by yourself. Always stay close to your parents when you are in a store. Stay with your friends when you are at a playground.

There are many people who want to keep you safe. Make sure you always stay close to them!

Playing with a group of friends is fun and can help keep you safe.

GLOSSARY

abduct (ab-DUHKT) to take a person away when he or she doesn't want to go

defend (di-FEND) fight back against someone who is trying to hurt you

escape (i-SKAPE) get away

lure (LOOR) trick someone into coming closer

reply (ri-PLYE) answer

stranger (STRAYN-jur) a person you do not know

FIND OUT MORE

BOOKS

Ferguson, Sarah, Duchess of York. *Ashley Learns About Strangers*. New York: Sterling, 2010.

Joyce, Irma. *Never Talk to Strangers*. New York: Random House, 2009.

Petty, Kate, Lisa Kopper, and Jim Pipe. *Being Careful with Strangers*. Mankato, MN: Stargazer Books, 2009.

WEB SITES

FBI—Kids: Safety Tips
www.fbi.gov/fun-games/kids/kids-safety
Play fun games and read safety tips for dealing with strangers on the Internet.

McGruff.org—Strangers and Other Dangers
www.mcgruff.org/Advice/stranger_danger.php
Read some more tips for dealing with strangers.

INDEX

ABOUT THE AUTHOR

Wil Mara is the award-winning author of more than 120 books, many of which are educational titles for children. More information about his work can be found at *www.wilmara.com.*

24